How to Improve Business with Tourism Marketing

Practical guide with effective tips

G. Dellis

Copyright © 2024

Guide to Tourism Marketing

Copyright © 2024

1. Introduction

Tourism marketing is a discipline focused on developing and managing promotional and communication activities aimed at boosting tourism in a specific geographical area. This sector is crucial for the economy of many countries, as tourism represents a significant source of income and employment.

The introduction to tourism marketing includes a series of concepts and strategies that can be used to attract tourists and promote tourist destinations. In this context, it is essential to identify the target audience, i.e., the public to whom marketing actions are directed, and to define the objectives to be achieved.

Moreover, tourism marketing also involves analyzing the market to identify tourist trends and preferences, so as to offer products and services that meet their needs. This process includes identifying the distinctive features of the tourist destination, evaluating the competition, and defining effective communication strategies.

One of the key elements of tourism marketing is creating a strong and recognizable brand that can differentiate the tourist destination from others and convey a positive and consistent image. Therefore, it is important to develop a branding strategy that includes designing a logo, developing visual communication, and defining a distinctive tone of voice.

Tourism marketing also uses specific tools and techniques to achieve the set objectives. Among the most common are advertising, direct marketing, web marketing, and social media marketing. These activities can be carried out independently by the tourism body or entrusted to specialized agencies that plan and manage advertising campaigns.

Additionally, tourism marketing involves creating partnerships and synergies with other industry players, such as airlines, travel agencies, hotels, and restaurants. These collaborations can help expand the tourist offer and improve the tourist experience, making the destination more attractive and competitive in the market.

Finally, it is important to emphasize that tourism marketing is a dynamic and constantly evolving process, requiring continuous monitoring and adaptation to new trends and tourist needs. In this sense, it is crucial to be flexible and ready to modify marketing strategies based on public feedback and industry innovations.

The introduction to tourism marketing is a highly relevant topic for those working in the tourism sector, as it provides the knowledge and skills necessary to successfully promote a tourist destination and attract an increasing number of visitors. Through proper planning and implementation of marketing strategies, it is possible to increase the visibility and reputation of the destination and contribute to its economic and social growth.

2. Identification of the Target Audience

In tourism marketing, identifying the target audience is a fundamental step in creating effective and targeted strategies to reach the right audience. This process involves analyzing and understanding the characteristics, needs, behaviors, and preferences of potential customers in order to create offers and messages that attract and satisfy their needs.

To identify the target audience in tourism marketing, it is first necessary to define different market segments based on demographic, behavioral, geographic, and psychographic criteria. For example, market segments can be identified based on age, gender, income, profession, travel habits, destination preferences, and so on. This way, detailed profiles of potential customers can be created to better understand their needs and travel motivations.

Another important phase in identifying the target audience is analyzing the competition and the market. It is crucial to understand who the direct and indirect competitors are in the tourism sector, what their offers and strengths and weaknesses are, and what market trends and growth opportunities exist. This allows identifying competitive advantages and effectively positioning the offer compared to the competition.

Another aspect to consider in identifying the target audience is the use of advanced tools and technologies to collect and analyze data from potential customers. Thanks to the use of CRM software, data analysis, and social media monitoring, it is possible to obtain detailed information on customers' online and offline behaviors, their travel and purchase preferences, and market trends. This allows personalizing marketing strategies and offering personalized experiences to customers.

Finally, another important aspect in identifying the target audience in tourism marketing is segmenting the audience based on travel needs and motivations. For example, market segments can be created for customers seeking cultural experiences, for those desiring relaxation and wellness, for those preferring adventure and sports, and so on. This way, targeted offers and travel packages can be created to meet the specific needs of each market segment.

Thanks to a correct identification of the target audience, it is possible to create effective marketing strategies, offer personalized experiences to customers, and gain a competitive advantage in the tourism sector.

3. Competition Analysis

Competition analysis plays a crucial role in tourism marketing as it helps understand the competitive context in which a company operates and identify the main opportunities and threats in the market. This type of analysis allows identifying the strengths and weaknesses of direct and indirect competitors, as well as evaluating the strategies adopted by them to determine how to differentiate and position oneself competitively.

To conduct an effective competition analysis in the tourism sector, various aspects need to be considered, including the type of competitors present in the market (e.g., hotels, tour operators, travel agencies, online platforms), the level of service offered, the quality of the offer, the prices charged, communication and online presence, customer satisfaction, and reviews.

One of the most used tools for conducting

competition analysis in tourism marketing is the SWOT matrix, which helps identify the internal strengths (Strengths) and weaknesses (Weaknesses) of the company, as well as the external opportunities (Opportunities) and threats (Threats) from the competitive environment.

In the context of tourism marketing, the main variables to consider during competition analysis include:

1. **Tourist Offer**: It is essential to analyze the tourist offer of the main competitors in the market, evaluating the variety of products and services offered, their quality, and originality. It is also important to consider the competition's positioning concerning specific market segments (e.g., eco-sustainable tourism, cultural tourism, food and wine tourism) to identify possible market niches not yet covered.

2. **Prices and Commercial Policies**: Analyzing the prices charged by the competition and the commercial policies adopted (discounts, promotions, vacation packages) allows evaluating the company's competitiveness compared to competitors and identifying possible differentiation opportunities. It is also important to monitor the dynamic pricing strategies adopted by competitors and customer reviews regarding the price-quality ratio.

3. **Distribution and Communication Channels**: It is crucial to evaluate the distribution channels used by the competition to reach their target audience (e.g., travel agencies, online platforms, social media) and analyze the communication strategies adopted (advertising, public relations, experiential marketing). This allows identifying the best practices in the sector and finding opportunities to improve visibility and strengthen the brand.

4. **Online Reputation and Customer Feedback**: Monitoring the online reputation of competitors (through reviews on TripAdvisor, comments on social media, travel forums) allows evaluating the level of customer satisfaction and identifying strengths and weaknesses of the competitor's tourist offer. It is also important to analyze customer feedback to identify possible areas for improvement and to adapt one's marketing strategy based on market needs.

5. **Market Trends and Innovations**: Finally, it is essential to monitor market trends and innovations in the tourism sector to anticipate changes and promptly adapt one's offer. It is important to understand how competitors are evolving to remain competitive and identify new business opportunities to differentiate and gain market share.

The competitive context in which a company operates allows identifying the main opportunities and threats in the market.

Through tools like the SWOT matrix, it is possible to identify competitors' strengths and weaknesses, as well as the opportunities and threats from the competitive environment. Constantly monitoring the tourist offer, prices, distribution and communication channels, online reputation, and customer feedback allows identifying the best practices in the sector and adapting one's marketing strategy based on market needs.

4. Identification of Market Trends

Identifying market trends is a crucial aspect in tourism marketing as it helps understand consumers' needs and desires and anticipate future market demands. Market trends are influenced by various factors such as social, technological, and economic changes, and they can have a significant impact on the tourism sector.

One of the most evident trends in tourism marketing is the increasing demand for authentic and personalized experiences. Tourists are increasingly looking for unique and authentic experiences, away from the most touristy and crowded places. This has led to the emergence of new trends such as experiential tourism, which focuses on exciting and engaging activities, such as food and wine tourism, adventure tourism, and cultural tourism.

Another important trend in tourism marketing is the growing environmental awareness and the desire to travel sustainably. More and more tourists are attentive to the environmental impact of their travels and seek destinations and tourist facilities that adopt eco-friendly practices. This has driven many tourism organizations to implement green policies and initiatives to attract a market segment increasingly attentive to sustainability.

Besides the importance of sustainability, another relevant trend in tourism marketing is the increasing use of technology and social media. Tourists are increasingly using social media to plan and share their travel experiences, and tourism companies must be present on these channels to attract and engage their customers. Moreover, technology has revolutionized the travel experience, allowing tourists to book and organize their trips quickly and easily.

Another significant market trend in tourism marketing is the diversification of tourism types. Besides traditional cultural and beach tourism, more and more tourists are interested in new forms of tourism such as food and wine tourism, sports tourism, musical tourism, and experiential tourism. This has led tourism organizations to diversify their offers to meet the needs of an increasingly varied and interested public in new travel experiences.

In addition to these main market trends, there are also other emerging trends in the tourism sector that companies must monitor and adapt their marketing strategies accordingly. For example, the increase in experiential tourism, the growing popularity of food and wine trips, travelers' desire to explore unconventional destinations, and the demand for more flexible and personalized travel experiences are just some of the trends influencing the tourism industry.

To identify and capitalize on these market trends in tourism marketing, companies must be proactive in monitoring changes in travelers' behavior and adapt their marketing strategies accordingly. It is essential to have a clear vision of customers' needs and preferences to offer them relevant and engaging travel experiences. Moreover, it is important to be flexible and open to innovation to remain competitive

in a constantly evolving market.

Finally, another relevant market trend in tourism marketing is the increasing competition among tourist destinations. With the increase in international travel and the accessibility of means of transport, tourist destinations are constantly looking for new ways to attract tourists and differentiate themselves from the competition. This has led to the emergence of new marketing and communication strategies, increasingly targeted and personalized to reach the desired market segment.

Identifying market trends in tourism marketing is essential to guide the marketing strategies of companies in the sector and anticipate future consumer demands. Monitoring market trends and adopting innovative and sustainable strategies is crucial to remain competitive in a constantly evolving sector and respond effectively to the needs of today's and tomorrow's tourists.

5. Definition of SMART Goals

SMART goals are an effective methodology for defining business objectives that are Specific, Measurable, Achievable, Realistic, and Time-bound. This methodology is particularly useful in the tourism marketing sector, where it is essential to have clear and well-defined goals to maximize the success of marketing campaigns and promotional efforts.

1. **Specific**: Specific goals in tourism marketing are clearly defined and detailed objectives that indicate exactly what is to be achieved. For example, a specific goal could be to increase hotel bookings by 20% by the end of the year. This goal provides clear direction and a definition of success.

2. **Measurable**: Measurable goals in tourism marketing are objectives that can be quantified and measured to evaluate their success. For example, if the goal is to increase hotel bookings by 20%, it is important to have

clear metrics to monitor progress and determine if the goal has been achieved.

3. **Achievable**: Achievable goals in tourism marketing are objectives that can be reached with the resources and skills available to the company. It is important to set realistic goals that can be achieved with the available budget, personnel, and technologies.

4. **Realistic**: Realistic goals in tourism marketing are objectives that are achievable and attainable within the current resources and circumstances. It is important to avoid setting overly ambitious goals that might be unrealistic to achieve.

5. **Time-bound**: Time-bound goals in tourism marketing are objectives that have a clear and defined deadline. It is important to set precise times within which the goals must be achieved, to maintain the focus and motivation needed to achieve success.

In tourism marketing, SMART goals can be used for a variety of purposes, including increasing bookings, generating qualified leads, increasing online visibility, improving brand reputation, and much more. For example, if a tour operator wants to increase bookings for a specific tour, they could set a specific SMART goal, such as increasing bookings by 30% by the end of the quarter, measurable through the number of bookings made, achievable with a targeted promotional campaign, realistic based on current conversion rates, and time-bound within the established term.

Another example could be a local tourism body that wants to increase the online visibility of its destination. In this case, a SMART goal could be to increase website traffic by 50% within six months, measurable through site analytics, achievable with SEO strategies and social media marketing, realistic considering the competition and the sector, and time-bound within six months.

SMART goals are an essential tool in tourism marketing for defining clear, measurable, achievable, realistic, and time-bound objectives that guide the company's actions and strategies towards success. This methodology helps ensure that goals are achievable, motivating, and aligned with the company's broader objectives in the tourism sector.

6. dentification of Key Performance Indicators (KPIs)

Identifying Key Performance Indicators (KPIs) is a fundamental step in measuring the success of marketing strategies in the tourism sector. KPIs are useful metrics for evaluating the effectiveness of the actions taken and monitoring the achievement of set objectives. In defining KPIs, it is important to consider both short-term performance indicators, such as website traffic or conversions, and long-term indicators, such as customer lifetime value (CLV) or Net Promoter Score (NPS).

In tourism, marketing strategies can be aimed at various goals, such as increasing brand visibility, generating direct bookings, improving customer satisfaction, or fostering customer loyalty. For each objective, it is possible to identify specific KPIs that allow evaluating the success of the marketing actions taken.

Below are some categories of KPIs useful for measuring the success of marketing strategies in the tourism sector:

1. **Visibility Indicators**

One of the main objectives of tourism marketing is to increase online brand visibility to attract new customers and generate bookings. To evaluate brand visibility, metrics such as website traffic, search engine ranking (SEO), social media presence, and the number of visits generated by online advertising campaigns can be monitored.

2. **Conversion Indicators**

Another important goal is to generate direct bookings and increase the conversion rate of users into actual customers. Conversion-related KPIs can include the website conversion rate, cost per conversion (CPC), average booking value (ARV), and the percentage of bookings made directly on the site.

3. **Customer Satisfaction Indicators**

Customer satisfaction is crucial for fostering loyalty and positive word of mouth. To measure customer satisfaction, KPIs such as Net Promoter Score (NPS), customer retention rate, booking cancellation rate, and customer feedback collected through surveys or online reviews can be used.

4. **Loyalty Indicators**

Customer loyalty is a strategic goal for the tourism sector, as loyal customers tend to spend more and generate new bookings over time. Loyalty-related KPIs can include customer lifetime value (CLV), repeat booking rate, the number of positive reviews from loyal customers, and churn rate (the percentage of customers who do not return).

5. **Return on Investment (ROI) Indicators**

Finally, it is essential to monitor the return on investment of marketing strategies to evaluate the effectiveness of the actions taken and optimize resources. ROI-related KPIs can include cost per customer acquisition (CAC), revenue per available room (RevPAR), return on advertising spend (ROAS), and profit margin generated from bookings.

Identifying KPIs in tourism marketing is crucial for evaluating the success of marketing strategies and monitoring the achievement of set objectives. By using the right performance indicators, tourism companies can measure the effectiveness of their actions, optimize resources, and improve the customer experience. The choice of KPIs depends on the company's specific objectives and the characteristics of the reference market, but it is essential to define clear and measurable metrics to evaluate the long-term success of marketing strategies.

7. Creation of Brand Identity

Definition of Brand Mission and Vision

Creating a brand identity in tourism marketing is a fundamental process for distinguishing a company or organization from the competition and effectively communicating the brand's values, image, and personality to consumers. This process involves defining the brand mission and vision, which are key elements for guiding marketing and communication strategies and creating a unique experience for tourists.

Brand identity is the set of tangible and intangible elements that identify and represent a brand. These elements include the logo, colors, visual style, tone of voice, brand personality, and company values. Brand identity must be consistent and authentically reflect the company's mission, vision, and values.

The brand mission is the statement that describes the brand's fundamental purpose, its role in the market, and its commitment to customers and the community. The brand mission clearly defines the company's main objective and the reason for its existence, helping to create an emotional bond with consumers and differentiate from the competition.

The brand vision is the company's long-term vision, the dream that stakeholders want to achieve, representing the direction the company is heading. The brand vision inspires and motivates employees and helps guide strategic decisions for the future.

In tourism marketing, brand identity is particularly important because the tourism sector is highly competitive and saturated. Tourist destinations and companies in the sector must stand out and effectively communicate their unique features to attract and retain tourists.

Creating a brand identity in the tourism sector involves defining a brand mission and vision that reflect the desired tourist experience, cultural values, and environmental and social sustainability. These elements are essential for building a positive reputation, fostering consumer trust, and creating an emotional bond with the brand.

The brand mission in the tourism sector could be, for example, "Offering authentic and memorable experiences that enhance local culture and environmental heritage, contributing to the sustainability and well-being of host communities." This mission reflects the importance of creating a positive impact on visited territories, supporting local economies, and preserving the environment.

The brand vision in the tourism sector could be, for example, "Becoming the most sustainable and authentic destination in the world, recognized for warm hospitality, enhancement of local culture, and innovation in experiential tourism." This vision aims to position the brand as a leader in sustainable tourism and offer unique and meaningful experiences to tourists.

Brand identity in tourism marketing must be consistent and integrated into all communication and marketing activities, both online and offline. The logo, colors, visual style, and tone of voice must reflect the brand identity and convey the brand's values and personality authentically and engagingly.

Communication and promotion channels used in tourism marketing, such as the website, social media, advertising campaigns, and brochures, must be designed in line with the brand identity and the brand mission and vision. These tools must clearly and persuasively communicate the brand's advantages and values, stimulate tourists' interest, and encourage them to take action.

Brand identity in the tourism sector must be managed strategically and dynamically, considering market trends, consumer behavior, and competition evolution. Constantly monitoring the impact of marketing and communication activities on brand perception and tourists' purchasing behavior is essential for adapting and optimizing strategies and messages effectively.

Creating a brand identity in tourism marketing is a complex and strategic process that requires a deep understanding of the target audience, company values, and market trends. Defining clear and authentic brand mission and vision is crucial for guiding marketing and communication strategies, differentiating the brand from the competition, and creating a unique and memorable experience for tourists.

8. Creation of a Logo and Graphics Consistent with Brand Identity

Creating a logo and graphics consistent with brand identity is a fundamental element in tourism marketing. A well-designed logo can capture the public's attention and effectively communicate the essence and values of the brand. Moreover, consistent and well-curated graphics contribute to creating a professional and cohesive image, which can help differentiate the brand from the competition and build a positive reputation among potential customers.

When deciding to create a logo and graphics for a brand in the tourism sector, it is important to consider several factors. First, it is crucial to thoroughly understand the brand identity and the values one wishes to communicate. For example, if the brand is based on sustainability and environmental respect, the logo and graphics should evoke elements related to nature and environmental conservation.

Moreover, it is important to consider the brand's target audience. If the brand targets a young and dynamic audience, the logo and graphics should be modern and appealing. Conversely, if the target audience is more traditional and conservative, the logo and graphics should be more classic and sober.

Another aspect to consider in creating a logo and graphics for a brand in the tourism sector is consistency with other brand communication elements. The logo and graphics should align with the tone and style of the website, promotional materials, and advertising campaigns, creating a cohesive and recognizable image.

To create an effective logo that best represents the brand identity in the tourism sector, it is advisable to consult a professional designer with experience in the sector. The designer will be able to understand the brand's values and goals and translate them into a creative and original logo.

During the logo creation process, it is important to consider some key aspects. First, the logo should be simple but memorable. A too complex logo risks confusing the public and not being easily recognizable. Moreover, the logo should be suitable for use on various supports, such as websites, social media, printed materials, and promotional items.

Another aspect to consider in creating a logo for a brand in the tourism sector is the choice of colors and fonts. The chosen colors and fonts should align with the brand identity and the message to be communicated. For example, if the brand is based on nature and adventure, one might use vibrant colors and dynamic fonts.

Once the logo is created, it is important to develop consistent graphics inspired by the same elements and values. The graphics should reflect the logo's style and colors, creating a coordinated and harmonious image. Moreover, the graphics should be easily recognizable and distinguishable from other brands in the market.

In creating graphics, it is important to consider the different communication needs of the brand in the tourism market. For example, if the brand targets an international audience, it is important that the graphics are easily understandable even for people who speak different languages. Moreover, the graphics should be adaptable to various supports and formats, ensuring effective presence on all communication channels.

Finally, once the logo and graphics consistent with the brand identity in the tourism sector are created, it is important to monitor their effectiveness and impact on the public. Through market research, surveys, and analysis of customer feedback, it is possible to evaluate whether the logo and graphics are achieving the set goals and capturing the attention of the target audience.

Creating a logo and graphics consistent with brand identity in the tourism sector is a key element for differentiating from the competition, effectively communicating the brand's values and goals, and building a positive reputation among potential customers. Consulting a professional designer and considering all key design aspects are fundamental steps to ensure the brand's success in the competitive tourism market.

9. Definition of Brand Values and Personality

In tourism marketing, defining brand values and personality precisely and in detail is very important. The tourism sector is extremely competitive and saturated, so it is essential to have a clear brand identity that positions the company distinctively and competitively compared to competitors.

Brand values represent the fundamental ideals on which the company is based and guide all its actions and decisions. These values must be authentic and reflect the company's mission and vision. For example, if a tourism company has environmental sustainability as its main value, all its activities and offers must align with this principle.

Brand personality, on the other hand, is the way the brand communicates with its audience. It consists of various elements, such as tone of voice, graphic style, colors, images, and more, that together create a consistent and recognizable image of the company. Brand personality helps consumers identify the brand and feel emotionally involved with it.

To define brand values and personality in tourism marketing, it is first necessary to conduct a thorough analysis of the target audience. Who are the potential customers? What are their needs, preferences, and values? Understanding the audience is crucial to creating a brand that resonates with them.

Secondly, it is important to identify the fundamental values on which the company is based. These values can be related to sustainability, hospitality, adventure, culture, tradition, service quality, or anything else that characterizes the company and differentiates it from the competition. Once the values are identified, it is essential to communicate them effectively through the brand.

Brand personality must be consistent with the

company's values and mission. For example, if a tourism company has adventure and exploration as its main value, brand personality might be bold, dynamic, adventurous, with an energetic and enthusiastic tone of voice. This way, the brand will effectively communicate its values and stand out from the competition.

Another important aspect to consider in defining brand values and personality in tourism marketing is consistency. It is crucial that all brand touchpoints - from the website to social media, from the information office to promotional materials - reflect the brand's values and personality uniformly and consistently. Only in this way will a strong and recognizable image be created that will attract customers and retain them over time.

Finally, it is essential to constantly monitor the brand's performance and interaction with the public to ensure that brand values and personality are effective and resonant. In tourism marketing, where competition is fierce and customer needs are constantly evolving, it is crucial to be flexible and adaptable and have the ability to modify or revise brand values and personality based on new trends and audience needs.

Through a clear brand identity based on authentic values and a distinctive and consistent personality, a tourism company can differentiate itself from the competition, attract the right customers, and build a lasting relationship with its audience.

10. Choice of the Most Suitable Communication Channels for the Target Audience

The choice of communication channels in tourism marketing is a fundamental element to reach the target audience effectively and efficiently. The tourism sector is characterized by a great variety of targets, which can include domestic or international tourists, business or leisure travelers, families, young people, the elderly, etc. Each type of target requires a specific approach, and therefore it is essential to identify the most suitable communication channels to reach the desired audience.

The choice of communication channels depends on various factors, including the available budget, the type of message to be communicated, the characteristics of the target audience, and the communication objectives. It is important, therefore, to carefully analyze the audience being targeted and select the communication channels that guarantee the best result in terms of visibility, engagement, and conversion.

One of the most used communication channels in tourism marketing is certainly the web. The Internet has become a fundamental tool for searching information and booking trips, representing an ideal showcase for promoting tourist destinations, accommodations, attractions, and services related to tourism. Among the most effective online channels are websites, search engines, social media, and online booking platforms.

The institutional website is an indispensable tool for tourist destinations, offering visitors detailed and up-to-date information about the destination, attractions, events, special offers, and available services. A well-structured and user-friendly website can positively influence the potential tourist's travel decision, providing them with a pleasant and informative browsing experience.

Search engines like Google are fundamental to being found online by potential tourists. A good positioning on search engines can increase the visibility of one's website and generate qualified traffic towards it. It is important, therefore, to invest in SEO (Search Engine Optimization) to optimize one's website and ensure greater online visibility.

Social media are another important communication channel in tourism marketing. Platforms like Facebook, Instagram, Twitter, and LinkedIn allow direct interaction with the public, sharing quality content, promoting special offers, and creating a community of loyal followers. Images and videos are particularly effective on social media, as they stimulate the interest and emotion of potential tourists.

Online booking platforms like Booking.com, Expedia, Airbnb, and TripAdvisor are essential for accommodations, reaching a vast audience of travelers looking for accommodations and tourist services. Being present on these platforms increases the visibility and bookability of one's structures, reaching an international audience interested in traveling.

Besides the web, it is also important to consider offline communication channels in tourism marketing. Print media, television, radio, flyers, and billboards can be used to reach a broader and more diverse audience that might not be online. Events, tourism fairs, and guerrilla marketing activities are other useful tools for promoting tourist destinations and engaging the public creatively and emotionally.

Choosing communication channels in tourism marketing depends on a series of factors that need to be carefully evaluated to guarantee the maximum impact and effectiveness of one's communication strategy. It is important to identify the target audience, define communication objectives, and select the most suitable channels to reach the desired audience in a targeted and effective way. Only with a well-structured and personalized communication strategy can the maximum return on investment be achieved and success in the tourism sector.

11. Creation of Interesting and Engaging Content for Potential Tourists

Tourism marketing is primarily based on creating interesting and engaging content to attract potential tourists and encourage them to visit a specific destination. This process requires a deep understanding of the target audience, travel trends, and the experiences that can be offered.

To create engaging content for potential tourists, it is essential to have a well-defined strategy that takes into account the needs and desires of the target audience. This means knowing the market segments one is targeting, what their travel preferences are, their interests, and their motivations for choosing a specific destination.

Once the target audience is identified, it is important to create content that is relevant and interesting to them. This may include creating promotional videos showcasing the main attractions of the destination, articles telling exciting and engaging stories related to the place to visit, travel guides providing practical and useful information for planning the trip, and much more.

The content must be created with care and attention to detail, to capture the public's attention

and arouse their interest. High-quality images, captivating descriptions, and valuable information can be used to make potential tourists feel involved and eager to discover more about the promoted destination.

Moreover, it is important to use a variety of communication channels to disseminate the created content and reach the target audience effectively. This may include using social media, websites, blogs, newsletters, and other digital marketing tools to maximize the visibility and resonance of the content.

Another fundamental aspect of creating interesting content for potential tourists is the ability to tell stories that excite and engage the public. Stories have the power to convey emotions, create emotional bonds, and inspire actions, making them an important lever to attract and engage potential tourists.

For example, stories of travelers who have had extraordinary experiences in the promoted destination can be told, sharing their emotions, smiles, challenges, and successes. This type of narrative can help create an emotional bond with the public and make them identify with the told experiences, pushing them to desire to live the same emotions and adventures.

Finally, it is important to measure the effectiveness of the content created for potential tourists and make any improvements based on the obtained results. This may include analyzing engagement and conversion metrics, monitoring the traffic generated by the content, and evaluating user feedback.

Creating interesting and engaging content for potential tourists is a fundamental process in tourism marketing that requires creativity, attention to detail, and knowledge of the target audience. Through the creation of high-quality content, capable of exciting and inspiring, it is possible to attract and engage potential tourists and invite them to live unique and unforgettable experiences in the promoted destination.

12. Use of Influencers and Collaborations with Strategic Partners to Increase Brand Visibility

Tourism marketing is a constantly evolving sector where competition is increasingly fierce, and brand visibility becomes increasingly important to attract new customers and retain existing ones. In this context, the use of influencers and collaborations with strategic partners can be a fundamental lever to increase brand visibility and reach new market segments.

Influencers are people who have gained great visibility and credibility on social media thanks to their ability to create interesting and engaging content. Collaborating with them can be an excellent strategy to reach a wide audience of potential customers, particularly millennials and Generation Z, who are very active on social media and tend to trust recommendations and advice from people they follow and admire.

To make the most of influencers in tourism marketing, it is essential to identify those who best align with the brand's values and image, as well as with the target audience. For example, if it is a luxury hotel, it might be useful to collaborate with influencers who have a strong presence in the lifestyle and luxury travel sector. On the other hand, if it is a more informal and young tourist destination, it might be more appropriate to involve influencers related to the low-cost travel or adventure environment.

Once the right influencers are identified, it is important to establish a collaboration relationship based on transparency and authenticity. Influencers must feel free to express their opinion on the brand and the services offered, without being bound by rigid guidelines or pre-packaged marketing messages. In this way, the content created by influencers will be more credible and authentic, and more likely to be shared and appreciated by their audience.

Besides influencers, another important tool to increase brand visibility in tourism marketing is collaborations with strategic partners. These can be tour operators, travel agencies, airlines, transport companies, tourism institutions, and much more. Collaborating with strategic partners allows expanding one's network of contacts and reaching new market segments that would otherwise be difficult to reach.

To create effective collaborations with strategic partners in tourism marketing, it is essential to establish clear and shared objectives, as well as precisely define roles and responsibilities. Moreover, it is important that both parties benefit from the collaboration, both in terms of visibility and brand awareness and in terms of increasing sales and profits.

Furthermore, collaborations with strategic partners must be supported by an effective communication plan that includes the use of various promotion and marketing channels, such as social media, online advertising, events, and much more. In this way, the impact of the collaborations can be maximized, and brand visibility can be increased globally.

The use of influencers and collaborations with strategic partners can be an excellent strategy to increase brand visibility in tourism marketing. These two levers allow reaching a wide audience of potential customers, expanding one's network of contacts, and increasing brand awareness globally. However, it is essential that collaborations are based on transparency, authenticity, and the common goal of creating value for customers and the company. Only in this way can a lasting and positive impact on the business and brand reputation be achieved in the long term.

13. Creation of an Intuitive and Responsive Website

In the context of tourism marketing, implementing digital marketing strategies is fundamental to attracting tourists, increasing the visibility and reputation of a destination or a company in the tourism sector. One of the first and most important activities to undertake is the creation of an intuitive and responsive website.

An intuitive and responsive website is fundamental to offering users a pleasant and smooth browsing experience. This means that the site must be easy to navigate, with a clear and intuitive structure that allows users to easily find the information they need. Moreover, the site must be responsive, i.e., adapt optimally to any device used to access it, such as smartphones, tablets, and computers.

To create an intuitive and responsive website in the tourism marketing sector, it is important to consider some key elements. First, the site's design must be attractive and in line with the visual identity of the destination or company. The images must be of high quality and representative of the tourist attractions offered. Moreover, it is important that the text is clear, concise, and well-structured to provide useful and interesting information to users.

Another fundamental component of an intuitive and responsive website in tourism marketing is the presence of clear and well-positioned calls to action. Calls to action are buttons or links that invite users to perform certain actions, such as booking a stay, contacting the company, or downloading a travel guide. It is important that these calls to action are visible and easily accessible to users to guide them through the conversion process.

To ensure an optimal browsing experience for users, it is also important to optimize the website for search engines (SEO). This means using relevant keywords and optimizing the content to increase the site's visibility on search engines. Moreover, it is essential to consider users' needs and ensure that the site is fast, secure, and accessible, even for users with disabilities.

Finally, to ensure the website's success in tourism marketing, it is important to constantly monitor performance and make any improvements based on user feedback and marketing objectives. Tools like Google Analytics can provide valuable information on visits, user behavior, and traffic sources, allowing the effectiveness of marketing strategies to be evaluated and any adjustments to be made.

Creating an intuitive and responsive website is a fundamental step in implementing digital marketing strategies in the tourism sector. A well-structured, attractive, and optimized site can significantly contribute to attracting tourists, growing the business, and achieving marketing objectives. Therefore, it is important to invest time and resources in designing and optimizing a successful website capable of offering a positive user experience and generating tangible results for the company or tourist destination.

14. Use of Social Media to Promote the Tourist Destination

Social media has become an essential tool in tourism marketing, offering tourist destinations a platform to reach potential visitors, promote local attractions, and interact with the public in a direct and immediate way. Thanks to their wide reach and ability to engage a vast audience, social media has become a key channel for promoting tourist destinations effectively and efficiently.

Using social media to promote a tourist destination requires a well-defined and targeted strategy that considers the characteristics of the target audience, the main competitors, and the set marketing objective. It is important to identify the most suitable social media for one's sector and plan a content strategy that engages the target audience creatively and engagingly.

One of the fundamental aspects of tourism

promotion on social media is creating high-quality visual content that attracts users' attention and arouses their interest. Photos and videos of breathtaking landscapes, local tourist attractions, and outdoor activities are particularly effective in capturing users' imagination and encouraging them to visit the destination.

Moreover, it is important to create original and unique content that shows the authentic and genuine side of the tourist destination, avoiding clichés and stereotyped images often associated with the tourism sector. Telling exciting and engaging stories, sharing personal travel experiences, and offering useful tips and suggestions are all effective ways to engage the public and stimulate interest in the destination.

Besides creating original and visual content, it is essential to interact actively with the public on social media, responding to comments, questions, and reviews quickly and courteously. Direct engagement with users allows creating trust relationships and building an active and participatory online community that helps promote the tourist destination organically and authentically.

To increase the effectiveness of tourism promotion on social media, it is advisable to use targeting and segmentation tools to reach the specific audience interested in the destination. Thanks to the possibility of creating targeted and sponsored ads, it is possible to reach potential visitors who are already interested in the tourism sector and who could be influenced to visit the destination.

Finally, it is important to constantly monitor and evaluate the effectiveness of social media marketing activities by analyzing engagement, traffic, and conversion data to evaluate the return on investment and make any corrections or improvements to the strategy. Measuring results allows identifying the strengths and weaknesses of tourism promotion and optimizing future activities to maximize the destination's success.

Using social media to promote a tourist destination requires a targeted strategy, creative and engaging content, direct interaction with the public, and constant monitoring of results. Thanks to the ability to reach a vast audience quickly and effectively, social media has become an essential tool in tourism marketing, helping promote and enhance local attractions and stimulate travelers' interest in the destination.

15. Use of Online Advertising Tools to Reach a Wider Audience

Tourism marketing is a constantly evolving sector characterized by increasingly fierce competition and an increasingly demanding and informed public. For this reason, it is essential to adopt innovative and effective promotion strategies to reach a wider and differentiated audience. Among the various marketing strategies available, the use of online advertising tools has proven particularly effective in reaching a

vast and diversified audience, allowing the promotion of tourism services in a targeted and personalized way.

Online advertising tools allow creating targeted and personalized advertising campaigns, reaching potential customers based on various parameters such as interests, place of residence, age, gender, and browsing behaviors. This way, it is possible to reduce resource waste and maximize return on investment, increasing brand visibility and awareness and attracting new customers interested in the promoted tourist destination.

Among the most used online advertising tools in tourism marketing are social media ads, display ads, search engine marketing, and email marketing campaigns. Social media ads consist of publishing paid ads on platforms like Facebook, Instagram, X, and LinkedIn, allowing reaching a vast and diversified audience based on their interests and browsing behaviors. These tools allow creating engaging and attractive ads, interacting with potential customers in real-time, and monitoring campaign results to optimize them over time.

Display ads are visual ads published on affiliated websites and blogs, reaching potential customers interested in the promoted tourist destination while browsing the web. These tools allow creating attractive and personalized banners, monitoring the traffic generated by the ads, and measuring return on investment to optimize campaigns over time. Search engine marketing, on the other hand, consists of publishing paid ads on search engines like Google, reaching potential customers interested in the promoted tourist destination based on the search queries performed.

Finally, email marketing campaigns allow sending personalized and targeted communications to a list of contacts interested in the promoted tourist destination, stimulating interest and customer loyalty. These tools allow creating engaging and informative content, monitoring campaign effectiveness through analysis tools, and measuring email open and conversion rates. Moreover, it is possible to segment the contact list based on various parameters such as interests, preferences, and purchasing behaviors to send personalized and relevant communications.

Using online advertising tools in tourism marketing offers numerous advantages, including the possibility of reaching a wider and differentiated audience, increasing brand awareness and visibility, optimizing return on investment, and stimulating customer interest and loyalty. However, it is essential to adopt an integrated and coherent strategy that includes different types of online advertising tools and considers the characteristics and needs of the target audience.

Moreover, it is important to constantly monitor the results of advertising campaigns, test new strategies and approaches, and adapt marketing strategies based on the feedback received. Only in this way will it be possible to maximize the effectiveness of advertising campaigns and achieve tangible and lasting results in tourism marketing.

16. Constant Monitoring of Marketing Strategies' Performance

Constant monitoring of marketing strategies' performance in the tourism sector is fundamental to ensuring the success of promotional activities and guaranteeing a positive return on investment. In a competitive market like tourism, it is essential to carefully monitor the effectiveness of advertising campaigns, social media activities, promotional and communication actions to adapt strategies promptly and optimize results.

Monitoring the performance of tourism marketing strategies involves various phases and includes data analysis, result evaluation, comparison with set objectives, and definition of corrective actions or new strategies. The monitored data include website traffic, conversions, bookings, reviews, social media engagement, sales trends, and other relevant KPIs (Key Performance Indicators) to evaluate the effectiveness of marketing activities.

To monitor the performance of tourism marketing strategies, it is essential to use data analysis tools like Google Analytics to track and measure website traffic, conversions, user behavior, and other useful metrics to evaluate the effectiveness of online advertising campaigns. Moreover, it is important to monitor the performance of social media campaigns using social media analytics tools to evaluate user engagement, reach, interactions, and other performance indicators.

Besides data analysis, it is also important to monitor customer reviews and feedback using online reputation tools to evaluate customer satisfaction, identify any critical issues, and improve the quality of offered services. Online reviews are an important indicator of brand reputation and influence potential customers' purchase decisions, so it is fundamental to constantly monitor them and proactively manage any negative feedback.

Comparing the obtained results with the set objectives is a fundamental step to evaluate the effectiveness of tourism marketing strategies and understand if the implemented actions are leading to the desired results. If the results are not aligned with the objectives, it is important to evaluate the causes and define corrective actions to optimize the performance of marketing campaigns. In some cases, it might be necessary to rethink the entire marketing strategy and adopt different approaches to achieve the desired results.

Constant monitoring of the performance of tourism marketing strategies allows companies to quickly adapt to new market trends, customer needs, and competition, ensuring the maximum effectiveness of their promotional activities and a significant competitive advantage. In a dynamic and constantly evolving sector like tourism, it is fundamental to be flexible and ready to modify strategies based on the obtained results and new opportunities.

Finally, to ensure effective monitoring of the performance of tourism marketing strategies, it is essential to involve a competent and experienced team in data analysis, result evaluation, and definition of corrective actions. A data-driven approach and performance analysis allow companies to make informed decisions and constantly optimize their marketing strategies, ensuring the success of promotional activities and business growth in the tourism sector.

17. Data Analysis to Identify Any Errors and Strengths of the Adopted Strategies

Data analysis in tourism marketing is a fundamental process for evaluating the effectiveness of adopted strategies and identifying any errors to be corrected. This analysis is based on a series of data collected from various sources, such as surveys, market analysis, customer feedback, and performance analysis of marketing campaigns.

We start by analyzing data related to the tourism marketing strategies adopted by a specific destination. It is fundamental to evaluate the trend of bookings and tourist presences over time to understand if the marketing actions are leading to positive results. For example, it is possible to compare the number of bookings before and after the implementation of a specific advertising campaign or promotion to evaluate the actual impact on the business.

Another important aspect to consider is analyzing the communication channels used to promote the tourist destination. Through data such as click-through rate, conversion rate, and bounce rate, it is possible to evaluate the effectiveness of different marketing channels (e.g., social media, email marketing, online advertising) and understand which generate the most results in terms of traffic and conversions.

Moreover, it is important to analyze data related to customers' perception of the tourist destination and offered services. Through satisfaction surveys and customer feedback, it is possible to identify any areas for improvement and strengths to focus on to differentiate from the competition. For example, if customers particularly appreciate the quality of the offered service or the variety of proposed activities, this can be a strength to focus on to attract new customers.

Another important source of data to analyze are online reviews and comments on social media. This feedback provides valuable information on the perception of the tourist destination by visitors and can influence the brand's reputation. It is fundamental to constantly monitor these reviews and promptly respond to negative comments to manage any crisis situations and preserve the brand image.

Finally, it is fundamental to analyze data related to the competition to evaluate one's market position and identify new growth opportunities. Through comparative analysis of prices, offers, and performance of competitors' marketing strategies, it is possible to identify any gaps in the market and find ways to stand out and attract new customers.

Data analysis in tourism marketing is a complex but fundamental process for evaluating the effectiveness of adopted strategies and identifying any errors to be corrected. Through the analysis of data related to bookings, communication channels, customer perception, online reviews, and competition, it is possible to get a complete overview of the situation and plan targeted actions to improve performance and achieve positive results.

18. Optimization of strategies based on results obtained

Optimizing strategies in tourism marketing is a fundamental process to ensure the success of advertising and promotional campaigns. This type of marketing is based on identifying and segmenting the target audience, analyzing market data and user behaviors, as well as interpreting the results obtained through various promotional activities.

To achieve satisfactory results in tourism marketing, it is essential to adopt a holistic and integrated approach that takes into account the various variables that can influence the success of advertising and promotional campaigns. In this context, optimizing strategies is crucial to maximize the effectiveness of investments and ensure a positive return on investment.

The results obtained from various tourism marketing activities must be carefully and thoroughly evaluated in order to identify any weaknesses and strengths of the strategies adopted. Only through a thorough analysis of the results can areas of improvement be identified and necessary corrections be made to optimize marketing strategies.

One of the most commonly used tools to evaluate the effectiveness of tourism marketing strategies is data analysis. Through the use of specialized software and platforms, it is possible to monitor the performance of advertising and promotional campaigns in real time, analyzing metrics such as website traffic, conversion rate, average user time on site, email open rate, and so on.

The collected data must be interpreted critically and accurately to identify any trends and patterns that can influence the success of marketing strategies. For example, if an increase in website traffic is observed following the publication of certain content or the distribution of certain offers, it can be inferred that these elements are of interest to the target audience and therefore their dissemination should be enhanced.

Similarly, it is important to constantly monitor user feedback through customer satisfaction surveys, online reviews, social media comments, and so on. These data provide valuable information on customer satisfaction levels, preferences, and any issues encountered during the tourism experience.

Another important strategy to optimize tourism marketing strategies is A/B testing. This technique involves creating two versions of an advertising content, randomly displaying them to two different groups of users. By analyzing the results obtained from the two versions, it is possible to identify which variant is more effective and optimize the marketing strategy accordingly.

Optimizing tourism marketing strategies is not limited to the planning and implementation phase of advertising campaigns, but is a continuous and evolving process. It is essential to constantly monitor the progress of campaigns and make any necessary corrections in real time to maximize the effectiveness of investments and ensure a positive return on investment.

Optimizing tourism marketing strategies is a complex process that requires specific skills and constant attention to detail. Through data analysis, constant monitoring of campaign performance, and interpretation of user feedback, it is possible to identify areas for improvement and make necessary corrections to maximize the effectiveness of investments and ensure the success of tourism marketing activities.

19. Online Reputation Management

Online reputation management is a crucial aspect for any business, especially in the tourism sector where the decision to travel to a particular destination often depends on the information and reviews found online. Monitoring and managing reviews are essential to maintain a good reputation and attract new customers.

The first step is to constantly monitor major review websites such as TripAdvisor, Google Maps, Booking.com, etc. to keep track of the feedback left by customers. It is important to respond promptly to these reviews, both positive and negative, to demonstrate attention to detail and interest in customers. Responses to negative reviews should be diplomatic and focused on resolving the issue, showing a willingness to improve and ensure a better future experience.

Positive reviews, on the other hand, should be thanked and shared on your social media channels to further enhance them. It is important to encourage satisfied customers to leave positive reviews to increase your online reputation and attract a broader customer base.

In addition to monitoring and managing reviews, another important strategy for online reputation management is content marketing. This technique involves creating and sharing quality, useful, and interesting content for your target audience. In the case of tourism marketing, this may include publishing informative articles about local attractions, travel guides, travel tips, videos and enticing images of the destination, special offers, and promotions.

Through content marketing, you can enhance the tourism destination, promoting it effectively and attractively to potential tourists. This strategy allows you to position yourself as an expert in the industry, build trust with your audience, and differentiate yourself from the competition.

Furthermore, content marketing can be an excellent tool to improve your search engine ranking, increase the visibility of your website, and attract more visitors interested in the tourism destination.

In addition to monitoring online reviews and managing your reputation through content marketing, it is also important to monitor and manage your presence on social media. Social networks are a crucial channel to interact with customers, promote the tourism destination, and enhance the experience offered. It is important to be active on social media, respond to customer comments and messages, share interesting and engaging content, and interact with your community.

Online reputation management is a key element for the success of any business in the tourism sector. Monitoring and managing online reviews, responding promptly to customer feedback, using content marketing strategies, and promoting the tourism destination on social media are all necessary steps to maintain a good reputation and attract new customers. Investing time and effort in online reputation management is therefore a strategic choice to thrive in the tourism sector and stand out from the competition.

20. Collaborations with tour operators, travel agencies, and other partners in the tourism industry

Collaborations with tour operators, travel agencies, and other partners in the tourism industry are crucial in the tourism marketing landscape as they allow for expanding the visibility of a brand, accessing new markets, and offering complete and diversified travel packages to customers, thus best meeting their needs and ensuring them an unforgettable travel experience.

Tour operators, travel agencies, and other partners in the tourism industry are entities with whom it is essential to establish strong and lasting collaboration relationships, based on mutual trust and shared common goals. Through such collaborations, positive synergies can be created that enable more effective results in terms of tourism promotion, as well as increasing sales and visibility of the brand.

In particular, collaborations with tour operators allow companies in the tourism industry to have a broader geographical coverage and offer customers complete travel packages that include flights, accommodations, transfers, and activities, ensuring them a worry-free travel experience. Tour operators can group various travel offers and negotiate advantageous rates with local suppliers, thus offering customers the opportunity to save on the final price of the travel package.

On the other hand, travel agencies are important intermediaries between customers and tourist destinations, capable of proposing personalized solutions and advising travelers on choosing the destination that best suits their needs. Collaborations with travel agencies enable companies in the tourism industry to reach a wider and more diversified clientele, access new market segments, and promote their tourism offers effectively and targetedly.

In addition to tour operators and travel agencies, there are other partners in the tourism industry with whom beneficial collaborations can be established, such as accommodation providers, suppliers of complementary tourism services (such as local tour operators, tour guides, car rentals, restaurants, and tourist attractions), and industry associations.

Collaborations with accommodation providers allow companies in the tourism industry to ensure their customers a comfortable and quality stay, offering them the opportunity to book travel packages that include accommodation in hotels, resorts, bed and breakfasts, or vacation apartments. Collaborations with providers of complementary tourism services, on the other hand, enrich the tourism offer with unique and authentic experiences, such as guided tours, sports activities, excursions, food and wine tastings, and cultural events.

Finally, collaborations with industry associations represent an opportunity for companies in the tourism industry to access useful information and resources for the development and promotion of their activities, participate in promotional events and initiatives, and establish contacts with other industry operators.

To best promote collaborations with tour operators, travel agencies, and other partners in the tourism industry, companies in the tourism sector must adopt an integrated marketing strategy that includes the use of various tools and communication channels, such as advertising campaigns, participation in tourism industry fairs and workshops, creation of advantageous partnerships and agreements, and promotion of products and services through digital channels and social media.

Furthermore, it is essential to establish collaboration relationships based on transparency, reliability, and mutual professionalism, respecting the agreements made and ensuring a quality service to customers.

Collaborations with tour operators, travel agencies, and other partners in the tourism industry are an opportunity for companies in the tourism sector to expand their customer portfolio, access new markets, and offer complete and personalized travel packages to travelers, ensuring them an unforgettable and satisfying travel experience. Through positive synergies and strong collaborations, it is possible to achieve more effective results in terms of tourism promotion and increase the visibility and competitiveness of the brand in the global tourism market.

21. Participation in fairs and industry events to increase the visibility of the tourist destination

Participating in fairs and industry events is one of the most effective strategies to increase the visibility of a tourist destination and attract a greater number of tourists. These events offer a unique opportunity to promote the attractions, services, and tourism experiences of the destination, as well as provide an important platform to create business contacts, establish partnerships, and stay updated on the latest industry trends.

Participating in tourism fairs and events allows destinations to present themselves directly to the target audience and effectively communicate their strengths and tourism offers. During these events, destinations can set up promotional booths to showcase their attractions, distribute informational material, organize events and presentations, and interact directly with visitors interested in visiting the destination.

An active and well-organized presence at fairs and tourism events can bring numerous benefits to the destination, including:

1. Increased visibility: Participating in industry fairs and events allows the destination to gain greater visibility among tour operators, journalists, tourism operators, and the general public. Thanks to their presence at these events, the destination can be known to a wide audience of potential visitors.

2. Creating business contacts: Fairs and industry events are an important meeting point for tourism operators, tour operators, travel agencies, journalists, and influencers. By participating in these events, destinations can create new commercial partnerships, establish collaboration agreements, and expand their network of contacts in the tourism industry.

3. Promotion of tourist attractions: During fairs and industry events, tourist destinations have the opportunity to promote their attractions, services, and unique tourism experiences. Through the distribution of promotional materials, the realization of presentations, and participation in thematic events, destinations can attract the interest of visitors and encourage them to visit the destination.

4. Exchange of knowledge and best practices: Tourism fairs and events provide the opportunity to participate in conferences, seminars, and workshops, where current topics are discussed and best practices are shared in the tourism sector. By participating in these events, destinations can acquire new knowledge, discover new trends, and stay updated on the latest developments in the sector.

5. Strengthening brand image: Participating in fairs and industry events allows the destination to strengthen its brand image and

position itself competitively in the tourism market. An active and well-organized presence at these events helps to consolidate the image of the destination as a quality, authentic, and welcoming tourist destination.

To maximize the effectiveness of participating in tourism fairs and events, it is essential to adopt an integrated marketing strategy, which includes planning and preparation in advance, defining clear and measurable objectives, creating a consistent and engaging communication message, and managing business contacts and partnerships effectively.

Furthermore, it is important to carefully select the fairs and events to participate in, evaluating their target audience, relevance to the destination, and potential impact on the market. It is advisable to participate in international industry fairs and events that attract an international audience and allow destinations to reach a broader audience of potential visitors.

Finally, to reap the maximum benefits from participating in tourism fairs and events, it is important to constantly monitor and evaluate the results obtained in order to measure the return on investment and make any necessary corrections or improvements to the marketing strategy. With active and strategic participation in tourism fairs and events, destinations can increase their visibility, attract new visitors, and consolidate their position in the tourism market.

22. Development of tourist packages and special offers to attract new customers

Tourism is one of the most important sectors of the global economy, with millions of people traveling around the world every year to explore new destinations, discover different cultures, and create unforgettable memories. With increasing competition in the tourism sector, companies must be able to distinguish themselves from other operators by offering tourist packages and special offers that attract new customers and encourage them to book with them.

Developing customized tourist packages and special offers is an effective marketing strategy to grab the attention of potential customers and stimulate demand for the tourist services offered. These packages can be designed to meet the needs and desires of different customer segments, offering unique and memorable experiences that set them apart from the competition.

To develop successful tourist packages and special offers, companies must consider several key factors, including market analysis, customer segmentation, competition evaluation, creation of authentic experiences, and planning of effective communication strategies. Furthermore, it is crucial for companies to collaborate with reliable suppliers and local partners to ensure the quality and reliability of the services offered.

Market analysis is the starting point for the development of tourist packages and special offers, as it allows companies to identify travel trends, customer preferences, and market opportunities. Through in-depth market research and analysis of demographic and behavioral data, companies can identify the most profitable customer segments and tailor their products and services to meet the specific needs of these customer groups.

Once the target customer segments are identified, companies can develop customized tourist packages that offer unique and memorable experiences that meet customer expectations. These packages can include a variety of services and activities, such as guided tours, excursions, cultural activities, culinary experiences, and luxury accommodations, designed to meet the needs and tastes of different customer segments.

Special offers, such as discounts, promotional packages, and last-minute deals, are another effective tool to attract new customers and incentivize bookings. These offers can be designed to stimulate demand during low seasons, increase loyalty among existing customers, and promote new destinations or tourist services. Companies can use various communication channels, such as websites, social media, online and offline advertising, to promote their special offers and reach a wider audience of potential customers.

Competition evaluation is another important aspect to consider in the development of tourist packages and special offers, as it allows companies to identify the strengths and weaknesses of their competitors and position their products and services uniquely and differently in the market. Studying competitors' pricing, promotion, and distribution strategies can help companies identify opportunities for improvement and innovation to attract new customers and increase their market share.

Creating authentic and engaging experiences is crucial for the success of tourist packages and special offers, as it allows companies to differentiate themselves and create an emotional bond with customers. Authentic experiences can include personalized guided tours, interactions with the local population, authentic culinary and cultural experiences, offering customers a unique opportunity to explore and experience the destination authentically and meaningfully.

Finally, the development of tourist packages and special offers requires strategic planning and effective communication to ensure the success of marketing initiatives. Companies must carefully plan timing, distribution channels, and marketing messages to reach the target audience at the right time and in the most effective way. Also, it is crucial to constantly monitor and evaluate the performance of marketing initiatives to identify best practices and adapt strategies based on customer feedback and market trends.

The development of tourist packages and special offers represents an effective marketing strategy to attract new customers and increase the profitability of companies in the tourism sector. Identifying target customer segments, creating authentic and engaging experiences, evaluating competition, and planning effective communication strategies are crucial for the success of marketing initiatives in the tourism sector. By collaborating with reliable partners and offering quality services, companies can differentiate themselves from the competition and add value for their customers, creating unforgettable and lasting travel experiences.

23. Evaluation of ROI

Calculating Return on Investment (ROI) is one of the most important concepts in the field of marketing, particularly in the tourism sector. ROI is a key indicator that measures the efficiency and profitability of an investment, showing how much money has been earned or lost relative to the initial investment.

In a highly competitive industry like tourism, it is crucial to carefully evaluate the ROI of marketing strategies implemented to maximize returns on every euro invested. In this context, decisions based on concrete data and detailed cost-benefit analysis are essential for the success of a tourism business.

First and foremost, it is essential to clearly identify the objectives of tourism marketing and establish Key Performance Indicators (KPIs) that will be used to measure the success of these strategies. These KPIs may include visitor numbers, conversion rates, average booking value, customer retention rates, and so on. Once the objectives and KPIs are defined, the effectiveness of marketing strategies can be evaluated through ROI calculation.

Calculating ROI in tourism marketing involves two fundamental elements: investment costs and benefits received. Investment costs may include advertising budgets, promotional expenses, production costs of promotional materials, expenses for industry events and fairs, intermediary commissions, and so on. On the other hand, benefits received can be represented by direct revenues (e.g., bookings received through marketing strategies) and indirect benefits such as increased brand awareness, improved online reputation, and increased customer loyalty.

Once costs and benefits are identified, ROI can be calculated using the following formula:

(Revenue – Costs) / Costs x 100 = ROI (%)

For example, if a tourism business invested 10,000 euros in a marketing campaign that resulted in a booking increase worth 25,000 euros, the ROI would be calculated as follows:

$(25,000 - 10,000) / 10,000 \times 100 = 150\%$

In this case, the ROI would be 150%, meaning that for every euro invested in the marketing campaign, the business gained a profit of 150%. This is a very positive result indicating that the marketing strategy adopted was highly effective.

After calculating the ROI of tourism marketing strategies, it is important to analyze the results and make changes to strategies to maximize ROI. If the ROI is positive, it is crucial to understand the key elements of the strategy's success and replicate them in future campaigns. On the other hand, if the ROI is negative, it is necessary to identify the causes of failure and make necessary changes to improve performance.

Changes to marketing strategies can involve different aspects such as audience targeting, communication messaging, distribution channels used, promotional offers, and more. It is important to test these changes and constantly monitor performance to ensure they are producing desired results.

Another important aspect to consider in evaluating ROI in tourism marketing is the duration of the effect of adopted strategies. Some marketing strategies may generate immediate benefits, such as increased bookings during a promotional campaign, while others may generate long-term benefits, like increased customer loyalty over time.

Therefore, it is important to assess ROI in the short and long term to have a comprehensive view of the effectiveness of marketing strategies. This will allow tourism businesses to effectively plan their strategies and achieve sustainable results over time.

Evaluation of ROI in tourism marketing is a fundamental process to measure the effectiveness of adopted marketing strategies and maximize results. Through careful analysis of costs and benefits, key aspects of success can be identified, and necessary changes can be made to improve performance. Constantly monitoring ROI in the short and long term will enable tourism businesses to maintain a competitive advantage in the market and achieve their business goals.

24. Glossary of Tourism Marketing

Tourism marketing is a fundamental sector for promoting tourist destinations, attracting travelers, and increasing tourism in a specific geographic area. To fully understand the world of tourism marketing, it is important to know some key terms that are used daily in the industry. Below you will find a comprehensive glossary that will allow you to better understand the language used in tourism marketing.

1. Tourist attractions: These are places, monuments, events, or activities that attract tourists to a particular destination. They can be natural, cultural, historical, etc.

2. Tourist: A person who travels for pleasure or for work to a location other than their residence.

3. Tourist destination: A place or region that

offers attractions, services, and infrastructure to accommodate tourists.

4. Market segmentation: The process of dividing potential customers into homogeneous groups based on demographic, behavioral, geographic characteristics, etc.

5. Positioning: How a tourist destination differentiates itself from others and communicates its uniqueness to potential tourists.

6. Branding: Creating and managing the brand image of a tourist destination to attract and retain tourists.

7. Advertising: Promotion through paid communication channels to reach a wider audience.

8. Promotion: Communication activity aimed

at promoting a tourist destination and encouraging bookings.

9. Experiential marketing: an extension of tourism marketing that emphasizes the tourist experience as the main added value.

10. Sustainable tourism: The type of tourism that is committed to reducing environmental impact, promoting the conservation of cultural heritage, and offering benefits to local communities.

11. Tourism events: Events organized to attract tourists to a particular destination.

12. Food and wine tourism: A form of tourism focused on the discovery and tasting of local culinary and wine specialties.

13. Cultural tourism: A type of tourism that focuses on exploring cultural, historical, and

artistic sites.

14. Luxury tourism: A market segment that targets travelers seeking exclusive travel experiences, high-quality services, and comfort.

15. Religious tourism: A form of tourism that focuses on destinations and religious practices.

16. Adventure tourism: A mode of travel that involves adventurous and engaging activities such as hikes, trekking, rafting, etc.

17. Distribution channel: The way in which tourist services are offered and sold to the customer, such as travel agencies, tour operators, websites, etc.

18. Revenue management: Revenue management strategy in the tourism sector that

aims to maximize earnings through rate and availability control.

19. Digital marketing: The use of digital tools and platforms to promote a tourist destination and reach potential tourists online.

20. Social media marketing: The use of social media to promote a tourist destination, interact with tourists, and create an emotional connection with the audience.

21. SEO (Search Engine Optimization): Search engine optimization to improve the positioning of a tourist destination on search results.

22. SEM (Search Engine Marketing): Paid marketing strategies to promote a tourist destination on search engines.

23. Google Analytics: Web analysis tool to

monitor traffic on a tourist destination website and measure the performance of marketing campaigns.

24. Content marketing: Creation and distribution of informative, educational, or entertaining content to attract and engage potential tourists.

25. Influencer marketing: Collaboration with influencers or celebrities to promote a tourist destination and reach new audiences.

26. Email marketing: the use of emails to send offers, promotions, and informative content to interested tourists.

27. Geomarketing: the use of geographic information to promote a tourist destination and customize offers based on the tourist's location.

28. Mobile marketing: Marketing strategies optimized for mobile devices, such as smartphones and tablets, to reach tourists effectively.

29. Inbound marketing: A marketing strategy that aims to attract tourists through the creation of valuable content, rather than interrupting their journey with intrusive ads.

30. Customer journey: The path a tourist takes from inspiration to booking, through research, evaluation of options, and the travel experience.

31. Call to action: A call to action that encourages the tourist to take a specific action, such as booking a trip, signing up for a newsletter, etc.

32. Customer relationship management (CRM): Customer relationship management to create loyalty and personalize the travel

experience.

33. User-generated content (UGC): User-generated content, such as reviews, photos, videos, that contribute to promoting a tourist destination through the direct experience of tourists.

34. Loyalty program: A loyalty program that rewards frequent tourists with discounts, exclusive benefits, or special experiences.

35. Reputation management: Managing the online reputation of a tourist destination to monitor reviews and tourist opinions and maintain a good image.

36. Benchmarking: Comparing the performance of a tourist destination with competitors to identify strengths and areas for improvement.

37. Tourism information center: A tourist information point that provides assistance, maps, guides, and advice to tourists visiting a destination.

38. Tour operator: Travel agency specialized in designing and selling complete tour packages, including transportation, accommodation, excursions, etc.

39. GDS (Global Distribution System): Global reservation system used by travel agencies and tour operators to access rates and availability of tourism services.

40. Yield management: Revenue management based on price and availability variations to maximize profits in the tourism sector.

Understanding these definitions will allow you to deepen your knowledge of the industry and develop effective marketing strategies to promote a tourist destination. It is important to stay updated on industry trends and news to adapt to the needs of tourists and offer unique and memorable experiences.

Index

1. Introduction pg.4

2. Identification of the Target Audience pg.9

3. Competition Analysis pg.12

4. Identification of Market Trends pg.17

5. Definition of SMART Goals pg.22

6. dentification of Key Performance Indicators (KPIs) pg.26

7. Creation of Brand Identity pg.30

8. Creation of a Logo and Graphics Consistent with Brand Identity pg.35

9. Definition of Brand Values and Personality pg.40

10. Choice of the Most Suitable Communication Channels for the Target Audience pg.44

11. Creation of Interesting and Engaging Content for Potential Tourists pg.49

12. Use of Influencers and Collaborations with Strategic Partners to Increase Brand Visibility pg.53

13. Creation of an Intuitive and Responsive Website pg.57

14. Use of Social Media to Promote the Tourist Destination pg.61

15. Use of Online Advertising Tools to Reach a Wider Audience pg.65

16. Constant Monitoring of Marketing Strategies' Performance pg.69

17. Data Analysis to Identify Any Errors and Strengths of the Adopted Strategies pg.73

18. Optimization of Strategies Based on Obtained Results pg.77

19. Online Reputation Management pg.81

20. Collaborations with tour operators, travel agencies, and other partners in the tourism industry pg.85

21. Participation in fairs and industry events to increase the visibility of the tourist destination pg.91

22. Development of tourist packages and special offers to attract new customers pg.95

23. Evaluation of ROI pg.101

24. Glossary of Tourism Marketing pg.106

www.ingramcontent.com/pod-product-compliance
Lightning Source LLC
Chambersburg PA
CBHW072052230526
45479CB00010B/686